CONTENTS

KV-639-113

Words that appear in **bold** are explained in the glossary.

FANTASTIC MACHINES

This book is all about things that go! Inside you will find amazing facts about some of the fastest, **BIGGEST** and most exciting machines in the world.

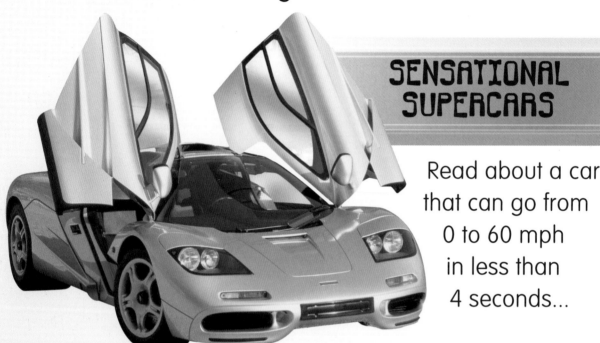

SENSATIONAL SUPERCARS

Read about a car that can go from 0 to 60 mph in less than 4 seconds...

SPEEDY SUPERBIKES

...a motorbike that can drive at over 200 mph...

MY FIRST BOOK OF

MACHINES

ÁLPARSVEIT SKÁTA REY

with thanks to
Frances Ridley

Caroline Bingham, Bill Gunston, David Kimber,

Richard Newland, Jeff Painter and Steve Parker

MY FIRST BOOK OF
MACHINES

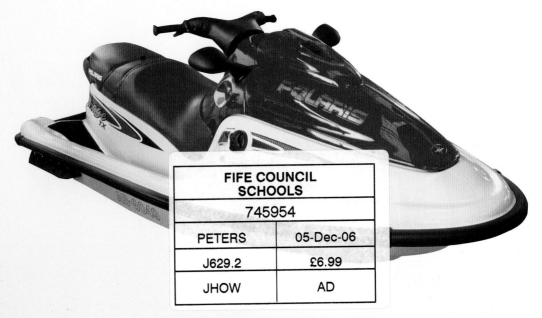

Copyright © **ticktock Entertainment Ltd 2006**

First published in Great Britain in 2006 by **ticktock Ltd.,**

Unit 2, Orchard Business Centre, North Farm Road, Tunbridge Wells, Kent, TN2 3XF

ISBN 1 84696 039 8 pbk

Printed in China

A CIP catalogue record for this book is available from the British Library.

Picture credits

OFC= outside front cover, t=top, b=bottom, c=centre, l-left, r=right
Ainscough Crane Hire: 32–33. Alamy: 78–79, 80b. Alvey & Towers: 28–29c, 46–47. Aviation Picture Library: 86–87, 88–89c, 90–91. Beken of Cowes: 58–59c. British Antarctic Survey: 54–55. Bronto: 68–69. Caterpillar: 40–41. Check-6 images: 80–81. John Clark Photography: 52–53. Corbis: 5t, 5ct, 30–31, 56–57, 59t, 60–61, 84–85, 89b. Sylvia Corday Photo Library: 77t. John Deere: 50–51. JCB: 44–45. Komatsu: OFC, 5b, 34–35, 38–39. Letourneau Inc: 36–37. Mack trucks: 30c. NASA: 92–93. Oshkosh: 5cb, 42–43, 48–49, 66–67. Peterbilt: 28c. RNLI: 64–65, 82-83. Robinson Helicopters: 70–71. Peter Slingsby Systems: 76–77c. The Car Photo Library: 4t, 4b, 6–7, 8–9, 10–11, 12–13, 14–15, 16–17, 18–19, 22–23, 24–25, 26–27.

US Coastguard: 72–73, 74–75. Yamaha: 62–63.

Every effort has been made to trace the copyright holders, and we apologise in advance for any unintentional omissions. We would be pleased to insert the appropriate acknowledgements in any subsequent edition of this publication.

BRILLIANT BOATS

...a boat that is as long as three football pitches....

POWERFUL PLANES

...an airliner that can carry 555 passengers...

EXCITING EMERGENCY VEHICLES

...a giant fire engine that fights fires at airports...

TERRIFIC TRUCKS AND DIGGERS

...and the biggest bulldozer in the world!

FERRARI

Ferrari is famous for making sports cars.
Ferrari had been making sports cars for 50 years
in 1996. They made a special car to celebrate.
The car was called the F50!

A Ferrari F50

The car's **body**, doors and
seats are made from **carbon fibre**.

The **exhausts** stick out of holes in the back – just like a racing car!

MACHINE FACTFILE

LAUNCHED:
1996

MADE IN:
Italy

TOP SPEED:
202 mph

ACCELERATION:
0 – 60 mph
in 3.7 seconds

WEIGHT:
1.23 tonnes

The **engine** is in the middle of the F50. It is nearly as powerful as a **Formula One** engine.

DID YOU KNOW?
The F50 can go from 0 mph to 150 mph in 18 seconds!

BUGATTI

Bugatti was once the biggest car maker in the world. The company was started by Ettore Bugatti. The EB 110 was named after him. The company shut down in 1996.

The car's **body** is made of **carbon fibre**. There were some bodies left over when the company shut down. They were used to make another supercar.

A Bugatti EB110

The EB 110 looks modern. But it has a wooden **dashboard** – just like an old sports car!

MACHINE FACTFILE

LAUNCHED:
1991

MADE IN:
France

TOP SPEED:
209 mph

ACCELERATION:
0 – 60 mph
in 3.4 seconds

WEIGHT:
1.56 tonnes

DID YOU KNOW?

Ettore Bugatti was Italian but he lived in France. He built his factory there.

JAGUAR

Jaguar made the XJ220S in 1994.

It was very fast. The XJ220S cost £293,750. It was much cheaper than other **supercars**.

A Jaguar XJ220S

The XJ22OS has a huge wing at the back. It is very wide for a sports car.

DID YOU KNOW?

When it was made in 1994 the XJ220S was the fastest road car in the world.

The car was based on a
Le Mans racing car. Le Mans
is a famous race in France.

MACHINE FACTFILE

LAUNCHED:
1994

MADE IN:
UK

TOP SPEED:
217 mph

ACCELERATION:
0 – 60 mph
in 3.3 seconds

WEIGHT:
1.08 tonnes

The XJ220S has a **body** made of **carbon fibre**.
This makes it very light

LAMBORGHINI

Lamborghini used to make tractors.

The company made its first **supercar** in 1966.

The Murcéilago is Lamborghini's tenth car.

The roof and doors are made of **steel**. The rest of the car is made from **carbon fibre**.

DID YOU KNOW?

The Lamborghini badge shows a bull. The bull is strong and beautiful – like the cars!

The doors in this sports cars open up instead of out.

MACHINE FACTFILE

LAUNCHED:
2001

MADE IN:
Italy

TOP SPEED:
205 mph

ACCELERATION:
0 – 60 mph
in 4 seconds

WEIGHT:
1.65 tonnes

A Lamborghini Murcéilago

The Murcéilago has **four-wheel drive**. This makes it easier to drive. It also has a special safety system. This slows the car down if it starts to skid.

McLaren

McLaren are famous for making **Formula One** Cars. They wanted to make the best **supercar** in the world. The result was the F1.

DID YOU KNOW?

The F1 was the fastest road car of its time! It was also the most expensive. It cost £634,500!

The F1's **engine** is huge.
It takes up all of the back of the car.

Each F1 car took nearly two months to make. McLaren only made 100 F1 cars.

A McLaren F1

MACHINE FACTFILE

LAUNCHED:
1993

MADE IN:
UK

TOP SPEED:
240.1 mph

ACCELERATION:
0 – 60 mph
in 3.2 seconds

WEIGHT:
1.14 tonnes

The F1 has three seats. It has one in the front and two in the back. The front seat is in the middle of the car.

MERCEDES-BENZ

Mercedes have been making sports cars for a long time. The Mercedes-Benz SL500 is a **convertible** sports car. The car's roof folds into the boot when you press a button!

A Mercedes Benz SL500

DID YOU KNOW?

The car has a sound system and a TV. You turn them on with your voice!

It only takes 17 seconds
for the car's roof to fold
into the boot.

MACHINE FACTFILE

LAUNCHED:
2001

MADE IN:
Germany

TOP SPEED:
155 mph

ACCELERATION:
0 – 60 mph
in 6.3 seconds

WEIGHT:
1.77 tonnes

The SL500
looks like the
old Mercedes 190 SL.
Elvis Presley drove a 190 SL in a film.
He was a famous pop star in the 1950s.

PAGANI ZONDA

The Pagani Zonda has a huge **engine**. Its roof is made of glass. The Zonda was named after a wind. The engine is made by AMG. They make racing car engines.

DID YOU KNOW?

You get a free pair of driving shoes when you buy a Zonda.

A Pagani Zonda C12 S

The Zonda doesn't have a boot. You put your bags behind the seats.

The inside is made of **aluminium**, **suede**, leather and **carbon fibre**.

MACHINE FACTFILE

LAUNCHED:
2001

MADE IN:
Italy

TOP SPEED:
220 mph

ACCELERATION:
0 – 60 mph
in 3.7 seconds

WEIGHT:
1.25 tonnes

This car's **exhaust** looks like a rocket. The car looks like a fighter plane!

TUSCAN

TVR are a company that makes sports cars in England. The first Tuscan was made in 2000. It is has a huge **engine**!

A TVR Tuscan

To open the door you press a little button under the wing mirror.

DID YOU KNOW?

When it was first made the Tuscan cost under £40,000. A good price for a sports car!

The roof and back window can be taken off! They will fit into the car's large boot.

MACHINE FACTFILE

LAUNCHED:
2000

MADE IN:
UK

TOP SPEED:
180 mph

ACCELERATION:
0 – 60 mph
in 4.4 seconds

weight:
1.1 tonnes

The Tuscan's engine fills up all the space under the bonnet!

THE FIREBOLT

The Firebolt is made by the Buell motorcycle company. It is very light for a **superbike**. Its powerful **engine** makes it really fast.

The Firebolt has a hollow **frame**. The petrol is pumped into the frame.

A Buell XB9R Firebolt

DID YOU KNOW?

Most bikes have chain to make the back wheel go round. The Firebolt has a belt instead.

The Firebolt has a big **brake disc** on its front wheel. It can brake really fast.

MACHINE FACTFILE

LAUNCHED:
2002

MADE IN:
USA

GEARS:
5

WEIGHT:
175 kg

TOP SPEED:
130 mph

The Firebolt is one of the lightest superbikes in the world.

THE HARLEY V-ROD

Harley-Davidson is famous for making motorbikes. Most Harley bikes are heavy. They are made for riding a long way. The V-Rod is much lighter. It is one of the fastest Harley bikes.

The V-Rod's fuel tank is under the seat.

A Harley V-Rod

DID YOU KNOW?

Evel Knievel was a famous stunt rider. He did all his jumps on a Harley-Davidson.

This special badge is on the fuel tank. It shows that Harley Davidson have been making bikes for 100 years.

MACHINE FACTFILE

LAUNCHED:
2002

MADE IN:
USA

GEARS:
5

WEIGHT:
270 kg

TOP SPEED:
135 mph

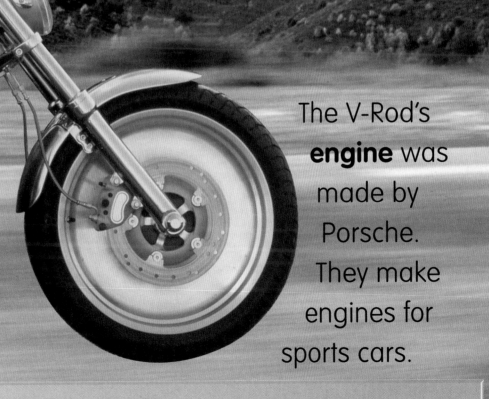

The V-Rod's **engine** was made by Porsche. They make engines for sports cars.

THE HAYABUSA

The Hayabusa is made by Suzuki. It is named after a Japanese hunting bird because it is fast and powerful.

The Hayabusa's **engine** is bigger than many car engines!

Suzuki GSX-R100 Hayabusa

Suzuki GSX-1300R Hayabusa

DID YOU KNOW?

A turbo-charged Hayabusa was recorded going faster than 241 mph!

The Hayabusa GSX-R100 has the same top speed as the GSX-1300R. But it has better **acceleration** because it is lighter.

MACHINE FACTFILE

LAUNCHED:
1998

MADE IN:
Japan

GEARS:
6

WEIGHT:
215 kg

TOP SPEED:
186 mph

The Hayabusa comes in blue, black and silver.

ARTICULATED TRUCKS

Articulated trucks are the biggest road trucks in the world. The front part of the truck is called the tractor. The back parts are called trailers.

The Peterbilt 379 road truck is an articulated truck. Peterbilt are famous for making trucks.

A Peterbilt 379 road truck

The huge **engine** is at the front of the truck. It is inside a long **hood**.

The hood tips forward. This lets you get to the engine easily.

MACHINE FACTFILE

PETERBILT 379 ROAD TRUCK

LAUNCHED:
1986

MADE IN:
USA

TOP SPEED: 130 mph

MAXIMUM LOAD:
25 tonnes

LENGTH:
6 metres

DID YOU KNOW?

Truck drivers may drive for many days. Some trucks have a bed in the tractor.

ROAD TRAINS

A road train is a truck that pulls three or more trailers. A road train carries huge loads from city to city.

A company called Mack makes road trains. The biggest Mack truck is called the Titan.

Mack trucks have a bulldog badge on the front.

Road trains have big **radiators**. They cool the engine down.

A Mack road train

MACHINE FACTFILE

MACK ROAD TRAIN

LAUNCHED:
1977

MADE IN:
AUSTRALIA

TOP SPEED: 60 mph

MAXIMUM LOAD:
120 tonnes

LENGTH:
53 metres

Road trains have big fuel tanks. They can go a long way before they need more fuel.

CRANES

Cranes are used to lift heavy loads. Some cranes are fixed in the same place. Other cranes are on wheels. You can drive them from place to place.

The Liebherr LTM 1500 puts down four legs when it lifts things.

DID YOU KNOW?

The biggest cranes in the world can lift 800 tonnes. That's the weight of six blue whales!

The LTM is on wheels.
It can lift the weight of 500 cars!

MACHINE FACTFILE

LIEBHERR LTM 1500 CRANE

LAUNCHED:
2002

MADE IN:
GERMANY

TOP SPEED: 50 mph

MAXIMUM LOAD:
500 tonnes

LIFTING HEIGHT:
175 metres

Cranes have a hook for lifting things.

A Liebherr LTM 1500 crane

A crane's arm is called a jib.

DUMP TRUCKS

Dump trucks are used to carry heavy loads **on site**. They do not go on roads.

This huge dump truck is made by Komatsu. It is called the Haulpak 930E. The wheels are nearly 3 metres tall!

A Haulpak 930E dump truck

DID YOU KNOW?
The driver has to climb up these stairs to get to the cab!

The truck works in **quarries** and **mines**. It carries huge loads of rock, earth and coal.

MACHINE FACTFILE

KOMATSU HAULPAK 930E

LAUNCHED:
1996

MADE IN:
JAPAN

TOP SPEED: 40 mph

MAXIMUM LOAD:
325 tonnes

WEIGHT OF EACH TYRE:
4.7 tonnes

The bucket is made of **steel**. Six big cars could fit in the bucket!

WHEEL LOADERS

A wheel loader digs up earth and rocks.

Then it dumps them into the back of a truck.

The wheel loader uses a bucket to dig.

DID YOU KNOW?

The L-2350 wheel loader has huge tyres. They are four metres tall. That's taller than three children put together!

The LeTourneau L-2350 is the biggest wheel loader in the world. A car could fit into its bucket.

MACHINE FACTFILE

LETOURNEAU L-2350

LAUNCHED:
2001

MADE IN:
USA

TOP SPEED: 10.5 mph

MAXIMUM LOAD:
72 tonnes

BUCKET WIDTH:
6.8 tonnes

The driver sits in the cab. He uses a joystick. The joystick makes the bucket dig and dump.

A LeTourneau L-2350 wheel loader.

BULLDOZERS

Bulldozers break up earth and push it around. The Komatsu D575A Super Dozer is huge. It is twice as big as any other bulldozer.

The Super Dozer's blade is 7.5 metres wide.

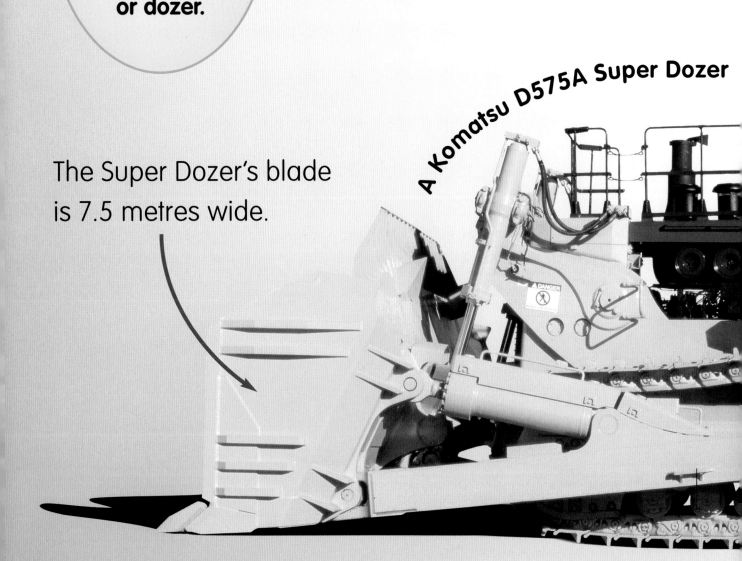

A Komatsu D575A Super Dozer

The Super Dozer has a Super Ripper! The Super Ripper can break up 2000 tonnes of earth an hour. Its teeth are more than a metre long.

MACHINE FACTFILE

KOMATSU D575A

LAUNCHED:
1991

MADE IN:
JAPAN

TOP SPEED:
7.5 mph forwards
8.3 mph backwards

WEIGHT:
76.54 tonnes

LENGTH:
15 metres

The Super Dozer has special tracks. They help it to go over muddy or bumpy ground.

EXCAVATORS

Excavators are digging machines. A company called Caterpillar makes lots of excavators. Some are small and some are large. The Cat 385L is huge!

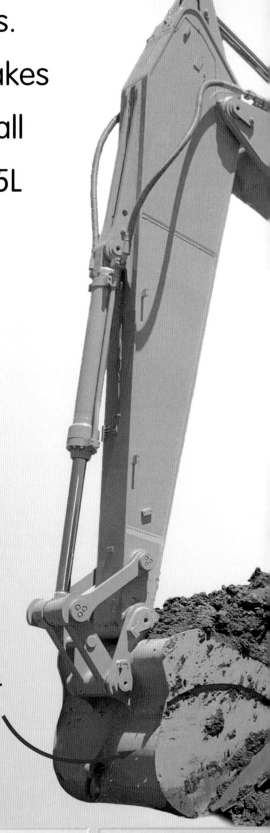

The excavator's arm has three parts. At the end is the bucket. The bucket has teeth that dig into the ground.

MACHINE FACTFILE

CAT 385L EXCAVATOR

LAUNCHED:
1991

MADE IN:
USA

TOP SPEED: 4.4 mph

HEIGHT OF CAB:
3.8 metres

WEIGHT:
83.5 tonnes

The cab is where the driver sits. The cab can turn all the way round.

A CAT 385L Excavator

The tracks help the Cat 385L to drive over bumpy and muddy ground.

MIXER TRUCKS

A mixer truck makes concrete. It mixes the concrete as it travels to the building site.

At the building site, the concrete is ready to use!

DID YOU KNOW?
Concrete is made from gravel, sand, cement and water.

This is an Oshkosh mixer. It sends the concrete down this **chute**.

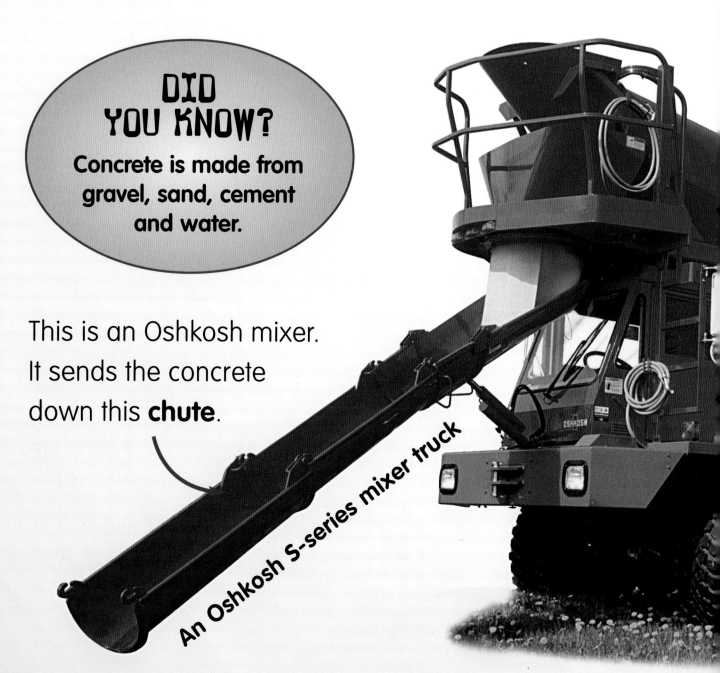

An Oshkosh S-series mixer truck

MACHINE FACTFILE

OSHKOSH S-SERIES MIXER

LAUNCHED:
1999

MADE IN:
USA

TOP SPEED: 50 mph

CHUTE LENGTH:
6.68 metres

LENGTH:
12.2 metres

This drum is where the concrete is mixed.

The drum turns round slowly as the mixer truck travels along. The drum is washed with water when it is empty.

BACKHOE LOADERS

A backhoe loader digs a hole with its bucket.

Then it picks up the earth with its **shovel**.

It moves the earth away.

This backhoe loader is made by JCB. JCB are famous for making trucks and diggers.

This is the shovel.

These are the Dancing Diggers! They do stunts and shows.

MACHINE FACTFILE

JCB BACKHOE LOADER

LAUNCHED:
1962

MADE IN:
UK

TOP SPEED: 67 mph

SHOVEL WIDTH:
2.35 metres

LENGTH:
5.62 metres

A JCB backhoe loader

This is the bucket. It can work at the back or the side of the loader.

RECOVERY TRUCKS

A recovery truck rescues broken down trucks.
The recovery truck fixes a winch on to the broken down truck. Then it pulls the truck to the garage to be mended.

This recovery truck was used to rescue army tanks. It has a huge **engine** and is very strong.

MACHINE FACTFILE

MERCEDES RECOVERY TRUCK

LAUNCHED:
1985

MADE IN:
GERMANY

TOP SPEED: 60 mph

WEIGHT:
20 tonnes

LENGTH:
12 metres

Sometimes recovery trucks rescue trucks at night.
They need very bright lights, like these.

A Mercedes recovery truck

SNOW MOVERS

Snow movers get snow off the roads. Oshkosh makes lots of snow movers. They move the snow in different ways.

This snow mover can push 5000 tonnes of snow an hour.

This snow mover has two **engines**. One engine drives the snow mover along. The other engine blows the snow out of the road.

DID YOU KNOW?

Some snow movers sweep the snow. Some blow the snow and some push it.

MACHINE FACTFILE

OSHKOSH SNOW MOVER

LAUNCHED:
1991

MADE IN:
USA

TOP SPEED: 45 mph

WEIGHT:
20.4 tonnes

LENGTH:
8.52 metres

The **exhaust** pipes go straight up into the air.

An Oshkosh snow blower

COMBINE HARVESTERS

A combine harvester works in a wheat field. It harvests the ripe wheat.

It cuts the wheat down. Then it strips the grain from the stalks. The stalks are left behind the combine harvester. They are picked up later.

This combine harvester is made by John Deere. The company's badge shows a deer.

MACHINE FACTFILE

JOHN DEERE 9750

LAUNCHED:
1999

MADE IN:
USA

TOP SPEED: 20 mph

MAXIMUM LOAD:
10,572 litres of grain

LENGTH:
10 metres

The grain is stored in this large tank.

These blades cut the wheat down.

DRAG BOATS

Drag boats are the fastest racing boats. They are more like rockets than boats. The Californian Quake drag boat can go at 230 mph!

DID YOU KNOW?
The Californian Quake can travel ¼ mile in under 5 seconds!

The top of the boat breaks off if there is a crash. This helps the driver to escape.

The driver's helmet is linked to a bottle of air. The driver can breathe underwater if he has a crash.

MACHINE FACTFILE

LAUNCHED:
1999

MADE IN:
USA

WEIGHT:
4.75 tonnes

LENGTH:
7.62 metres

TOP SPEED:
230 mph

The Californian Quake

Drag boats only hold one person.

RESEARCH SHIPS

Research ships explore new places. They find out all about them.

31 scientists work on the James Clark Ross research ship. The boat also carries 15 **crew**, 12 **officers** and a doctor.

The James Clark Ross

The James Clark Ross is a research ship in **Antarctica.** It finds out about the sea and the weather. It looks for strange creatures under the sea!

DID YOU KNOW?

The James Clark Ross can smash through thick ice!

MACHINE FACTFILE

LAUNCHED:
1990

MADE IN:
UK

WIDTH:
18.85 metres

LENGTH:
99 metres

TOP SPEED:
18 mph

The **hull** is made of strong **steel**. The ship is very heavy. It weighs 5732 tonnes – that's more than 30 jumbo jets put together!

FIREBOATS

Fireboats fight fires on ships and in buildings by the sea and rivers. Sometimes ships carry **cargo**, like oil, which can catch alight.

Six powerful pumps suck in water from around the boat. The water is fired out of water-guns.

A Los Angeles fireboat

All parts of the fireboat are **flameproof**.

2 LOS ANGELES CITY FIRE

MACHINE FACTFILE

LAUNCHED:
1925

MADE IN:
USA

WEIGHT:
152 tonnes

LENGTH:
30 metres

TOP SPEED:
20 mph

Fireboats don't spray water on electrical fires. They spray special foam instead.

DID YOU KNOW?

The boat's water-guns shoot jets of water as high as 150 metres.

AIRCRAFT CARRIERS

Aircraft carriers are warships. The Nimitz-class aircraft carrier is huge. It carries 85 planes and 6 helicopters. It also carries 6000 **crew** members!

Planes and helicopters need fuel. The fuel is kept in tanks. The tanks are the size of swimming pools!

DID YOU KNOW?

The crew of the Nimitz-class aircraft carrier eat 20,000 meals a day!

A Nimitz-class aircraft carrier

MACHINE FACTFILE

LAUNCHED:
1972

MADE IN:
USA

WEIGHT:
Over 100,000 tonnes

LENGTH:
333 metres

TOP SPEED:
35 mph

The crew use the latest computers and special machines for tracking other ships and planes.

The Nimitz-class carrier is as long as three football pitches!

OIL SUPERTANKERS

Oil supertankers are the biggest ships in the world. They carry millions of barrels of oil across the sea. The oil can be used to make petrol, paint and plastic.

This is the Jahre Viking supertanker. It has 40 **crew** members. They live in the stern.

DID YOU KNOW?

Oil supertankers are very slow. The Jahre Viking's top speed is 11.5 mph.

MACHINE FACTFILE

LAUNCHED:
1979

MADE IN:
Japan

WEIGHT:
564,763 unloaded

LENGTH:
458 metres

WIDTH:
69 metres

The oil comes from an oil rig. It is pumped on to the tanker through pipes.

The Jahre Viking oil supertanker

The ship's deck is huge. The crew sometimes use bikes to get around.

JETSKIS

You can ride a jetski over the waves at top speed. You can do stunts on them, too. The jetski stops if you fall off. This lets you get back on again!

The engine sucks water in. Then it blasts the water out in a fast jet. The jet pushes the jetski along.

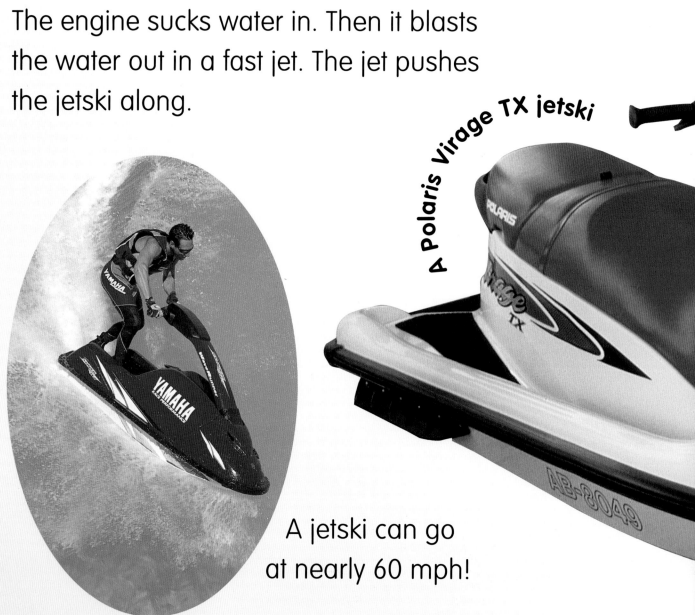

A Polaris Virage TX jetski

A jetski can go at nearly 60 mph!

MACHINE FACTFILE

LAUNCHED:
2000

MADE IN:
USA

WEIGHT:
285 kg

LENGTH:
3.06 metres

COST:
£8,000

You steer a jetski with handlebars – just like a bike.

LIFEBOATS

Lifeboats rescue people from the sea.
Lifeboats have to be strong and their **crews**
have to be brave.

The crew use radios
and special tracking
equipment to find
ships that are
in trouble.

The boat's **hull**
is made of plastic
and **carbon fibre**.
It is light and does
not rust.

DID YOU KNOW?

British lifeboats are called out about 17 times a day.

MACHINE FACTFILE

LAUNCHED:
1994

MADE IN:
UK

WEIGHT:
27.5 tonnes

LENGTH:
14.26 metres

SPEED:
29 mph

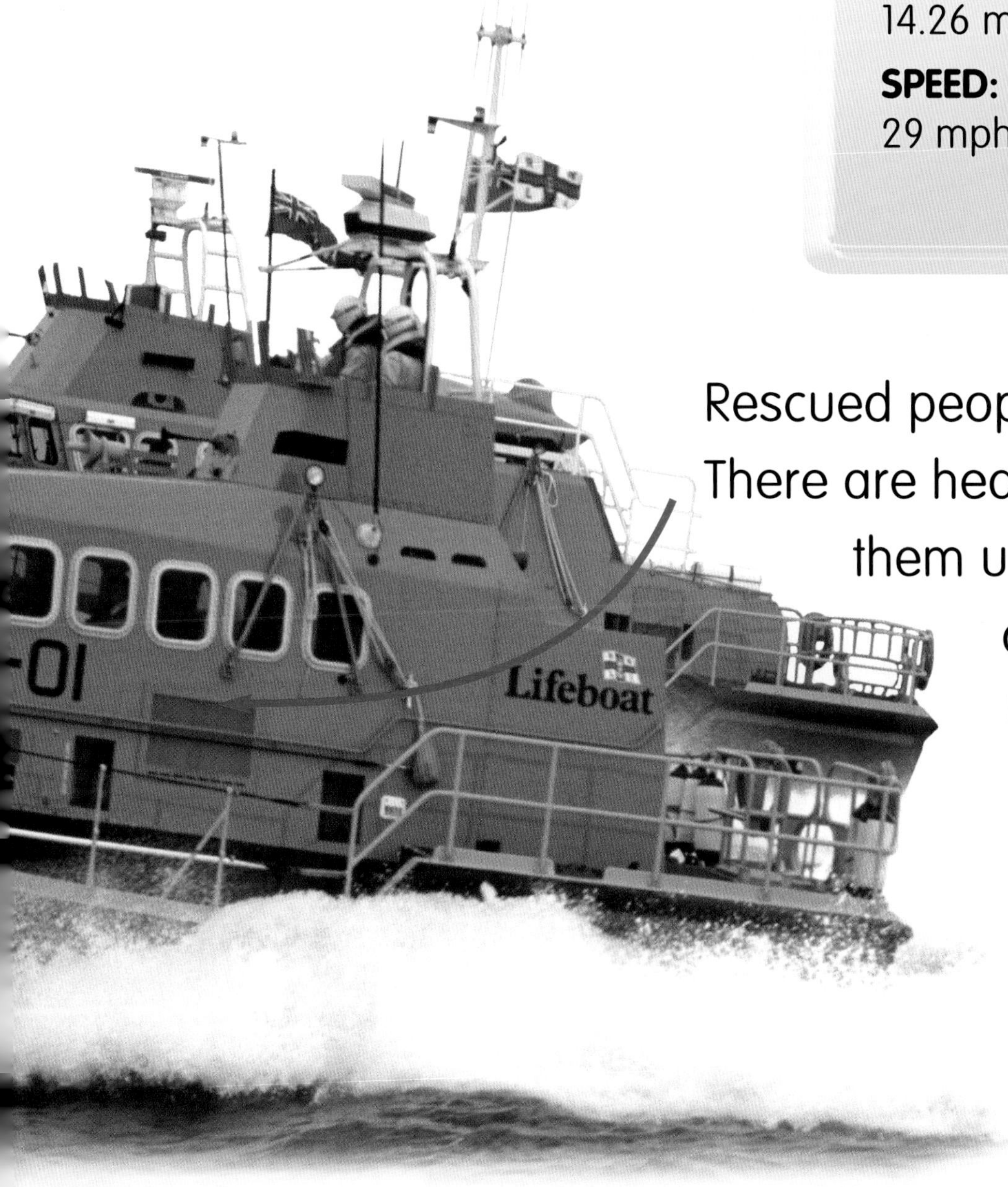

Rescued people sit here. There are heaters to warm them up. There are dry clothes, hot drinks and snacks.

THE STRIKER

The Striker fights airport fires. It is the biggest fire engine in the world.

The Striker makes a hole in a plane that is on fire. It puts a camera through the hole to see where the fire is. Then it shoots foam through the hole to put the fire out.

The Striker has huge wheels. They help it drive over muddy ground.

CENTRAL WISCONSIN AIRPORT

R1

DID YOU KNOW?

The Striker holds as much water as nine normal fire engines!

The Striker 4500 fire engine

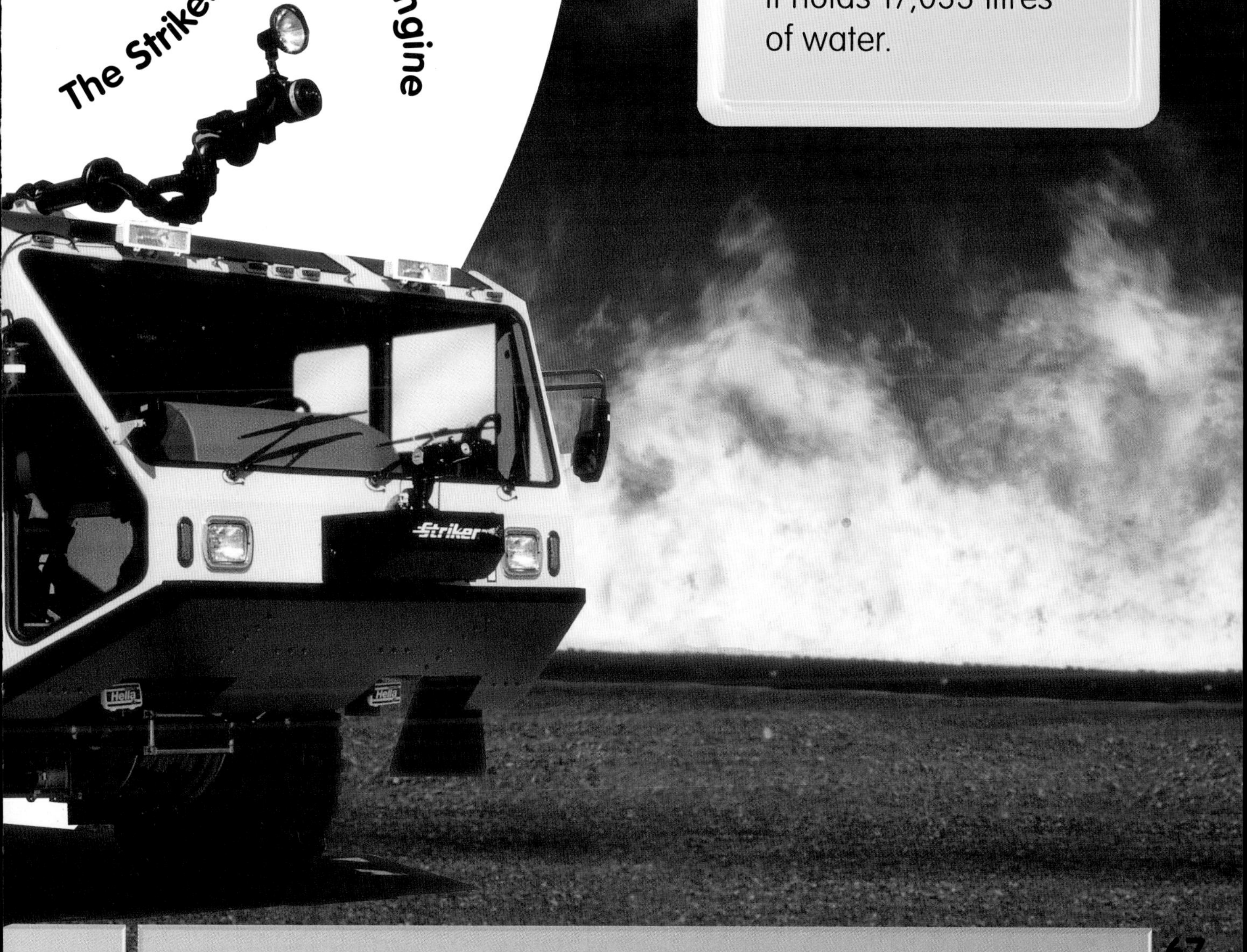

MACHINE FACTFILE

LAUNCHED:
2002

MADE IN:
USA

TOP SPEED:
50 mph

CREW:
5

AMAZING FACT:
It holds 17,033 litres of water.

THE BRONTO SKYLIFT

The Bronto Skylift is a fire truck. It has a platform on a very long arm. This helps to fight fires in very tall buildings. It helps firefighters to rescue people trapped inside.

The Bronto Skylift has a thick **steel** hose for spraying water. The hose unfolds with the arm.

A Bronto Skylift fire truck

BRONTO SKYLIFT F 88 HLA

ABOVE

DID YOU KNOW?

You can use the platform like a crane. It can lift someone out of a building on a stretcher.

MACHINE FACTFILE

LAUNCHED:
2000

MADE IN:
FINLAND

TOP SPEED:
40 mph

CREW:
5

AMAZING FACT:
It sprays 3800 litres of water per minute.

The Bronto Skylift can reach higher than any other fire engine. This model can reach 72 metres in the air.

R44 HELICOPTER

The R44 helicopter helps the police to do their job. It has a search light, a siren and a **loud speaker**.

The R44 helicopter

DID YOU KNOW?

The R44 has a special camera. It can film things on the ground when the R44 is flying.

Three people can sit in the R44. The big glass windows let everyone see out.

Helicopter **engines** make a lot of noise. The R44 is padded with special foam. This stops it being too noisy inside.

MACHINE FACTFILE

LAUNCHED:
1993

MADE IN:
USA

NORMAL SPEED:
130 mph

CREW:
2

AMAZING FACT:
The R44 files 4267 metres above the ground.

The R44 can go 400 miles on a full tank of fuel. That's very good for a helicopter!

AIRTANKERS

Airtankers fight forest fires.

They drop **fire retardant** on to the fire.

A P-3 Orion firefighting airtanker

The retardant is dropped in a straight line.
The fire won't spread over the line.

The P3's tank is under its body. The pilot uses a computer to open the tank's doors.

MACHINE FACTFILE

LAUNCHED AS AIRTANKER:
1990

MADE IN:
USA

TOP SPEED:
411 mph

CREW:
15

AMAZING FACT:
An airtanker costs about £1.5 million.

The P-3 Orion is named after a group of stars. The stars show a hunter called Orion.

AIR-SEA RESCUE HELICOPTERS

An air-sea rescue helicopter saves people who get into trouble at sea. It pulls them up on a line. Then it takes them to hospital.

6566

U. S. COAST GUARD

There is a small **blade** on the helicopter's tail. It helps the helicopter to stay in one place in the air.

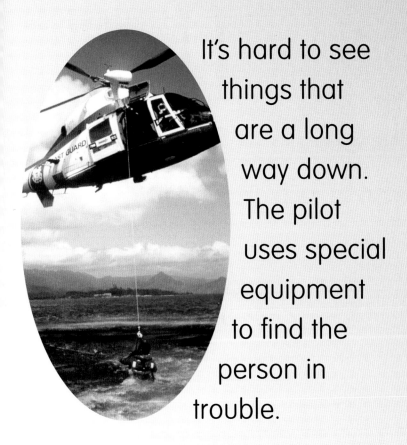

It's hard to see things that are a long way down. The pilot uses special equipment to find the person in trouble.

The HH-60J Jayhawk

The helicopter blades are 6 metres long. They are folded away when the helicopter isn't flying.

RESCUE SUBMERSIBLES

The LR7 is a rescue **submersible**.

It rescues people trapped in **submarines**.

The LR7 goes underwater and finds the submarine. It fixes on to the submarine. The trapped people can move into the LR7 through a special escape door.

LR7 RESCUE SUBMERSIBLE

DID YOU KNOW?

It's hard to see things underwater. The LR7 uses special equipment to find submarines.

The LR7 can rescue 18 people. They sit in the rescue **chamber** at the back.

This is the LR5 submersible. It is being lowered into the water.

MACHINE FACTFILE

LAUNCHED:
2004

MADE IN:
UK

TOP SPEED:
3.5 mph

CREW:
3

AMAZING FACT:
The LR7 is just 9.6 metres long.

The LR7 rescue submersible

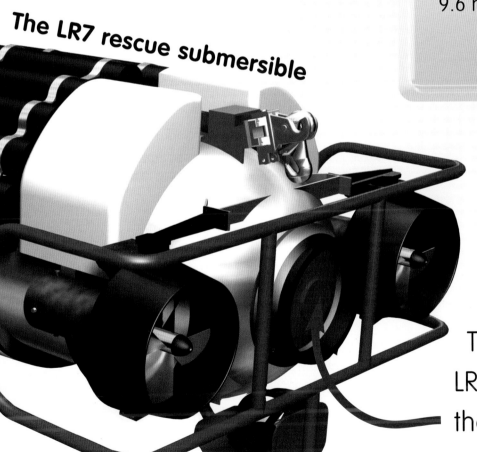

This is where the LR7 fixes on to the submarine.

HAGGLUNDS BV206

The Hagglunds BV206 does lots of different things. It fights fires. It rescues people. It explores deserts and jungles.

The Hagglunds BV206

DID YOU KNOW?

The Hagglunds can float, too! Its top speed in water is 1.86 mph.

The Hagglunds has special tracks. They can go over snow, ice, mud, grass or sand.

MACHINE FACTFILE

LAUNCHED:
1994

MADE IN:
Sweden

TOP SPEED ON LAND:
32 mph

CREW:
2

AMAZING FACT:

It can rescue and
carry 10 people
at once.

This vehicle has special tracks,
too. It rescues people trapped
in snow. It pushes the heavy
snow out of the way.

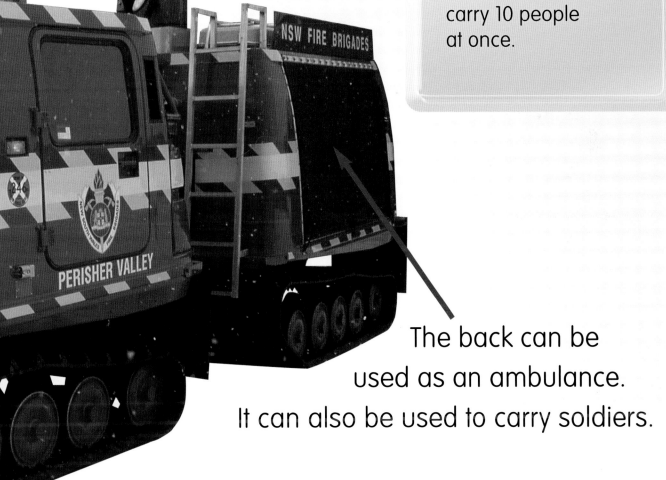

The back can be
used as an ambulance.
It can also be used to carry soldiers.

HEAVY RESCUE 56 TRUCK

This huge truck is owned by the Los Angeles Fire Department in America. It goes to accidents to do cutting or heavy lifting.

This arm can swing to the side to lift cars out of rivers or ditches.

A Heavy rescue 56

The winch has 90 metres of thick, **steel** cable.

The lifting equipment can be worked by remote control if it is too dangerous for the **crew** to get close to an accident.

MACHINE FACTFILE

LAUNCHED:
1995

MADE IN:
USA

TOP SPEED:
100 mph

CREW:
5

AMAZING FACT:
This machine can help lift up pieces of buildings that have fallen down.

DID YOU KNOW?

The winch is so strong it can lift something that weighs the same as 15 cars!

ATLANTIC 75 LIFEBOAT

DID YOU KNOW?

These boats are used to rescue people out at sea all over the world.

The Atlantic 75 helps rescue people out at sea. It has a hard, plastic **hull** and an inflatable section filled with air on top.

The inflatable part of the boat and the hull are divided into sections. This means if one section gets a hole, the boat doesn't sink.

If the boat turns over, the **crew** pull a cord. This blows up a big airbag which turns the boat the right way up!

MACHINE FACTFILE

LAUNCHED:
1992

MADE IN:
UK

TOP SPEED:
36.82 mph

CREW:
3

AMAZING FACT:
This boat can go 50 miles out to sea to a rescue.

The Atlantic 75 can keep travelling at its top speed for three hours before it needs more fuel.

AIRBUS A380

The airbus A380 is the largest **airliner** in the world.
It carries 555 passengers.

The Airbus A380 has three decks.
One deck is for the cargo.
The other two decks are
for the passengers.

DID YOU KNOW?

The Airbus A380-800F carries cargo, not people. It can carry 150 tonnes of cargo!

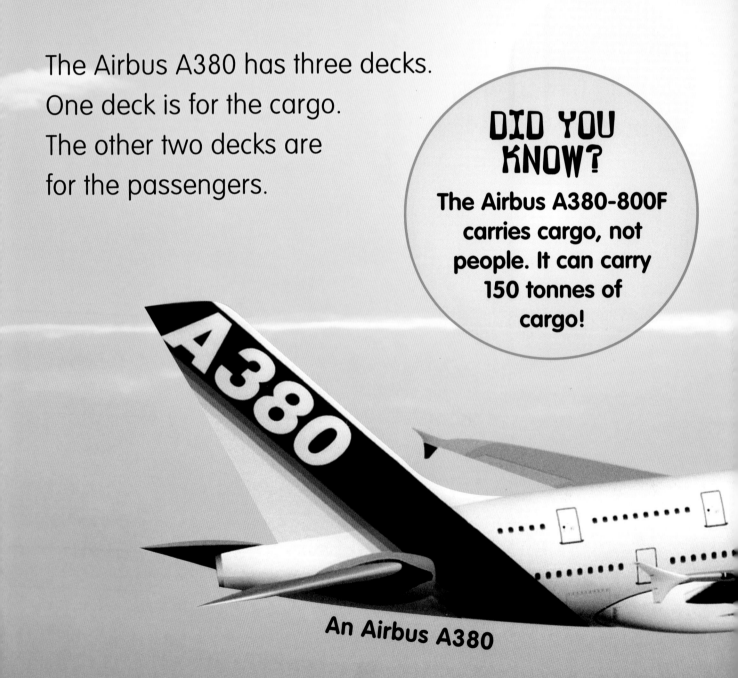

An Airbus A380

LAUNCHED:
2006

MADE IN:
Europe

WING SPAN:
79.8 metres

LENGTH:
73 metres

TOP SPEED:
647 mph

Passengers can walk around on the airbus. There are shops and places to eat. There are places for children to play, too!

The airbus has two **engines** on each wing.

THE BLACKBIRD

The SR-71 Blackbird is a spy plane. It has powerful **engines** and is very fast.

The Blackbird carries cameras and **sensors**. The cameras are used to spy on the enemy. The sensors are used to spot enemy planes.

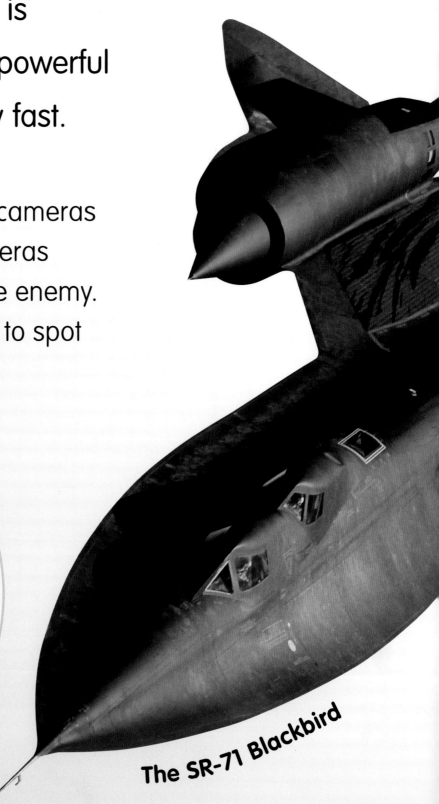

The SR-71 Blackbird

DID YOU KNOW?

The Blackbird flew from New York to London in less than two hours!

The Blackbird was made in top secret.

MACHINE FACTFILE

LAUNCHED:
1962

MADE IN:
USA

WINGSPAN:
16.94 metres

LENGTH:
31.65 metres

TOP SPEED:
2,250 mph

The plane is made from a special metal. It keeps the plane cool when it goes very fast.

JUMBO JET

The Boeing 747 is a big, fast **airliner**.

It is known as the jumbo jet.

DID YOU KNOW?

A jumbo jet carries 216,000 litres of fuel. That would fill up 4000 cars!

It can carry 412 passengers and 22 **crew**. It can also carry more than 100 tonnes of **cargo**.

The jumbo jet has four **engines** and 18 wheels.

MACHINE FACTFILE

LAUNCHED:
1966

MADE IN:
USA

WINGSPAN:
64 metres

LENGTH:
70.4 metres

TOP SPEED:
570 mph

A Boeing 747

The cargo can be loaded through the plane's nose!

THE TYPHOON

The Typhoon is a
war plane. It carries a gun,
missiles and bombs.
It goes faster than
the speed of sound!

A Eurofighter typhoon

DID YOU KNOW?

It took 20 years
to plan and
make the
Typhoon.

Most of the Typhoon's body is made of **carbon fibre**. It is much lighter than metal. The carbon fibre keeps the plane cool when it goes very fast.

Typhoons come with one or two seats.

LAUNCHED:
2002

MADE IN:
Europe

WINGSPAN:
10.95 metres

LENGTH:
15.96 metres

TOP SPEED:
1323 mph

These two **engines** make the Typhoon very fast. It can take off in five seconds!

THE SPACE SHUTTLE

The Shuttle is a space plane. It can be used again and again. The first spacecraft were only used once.

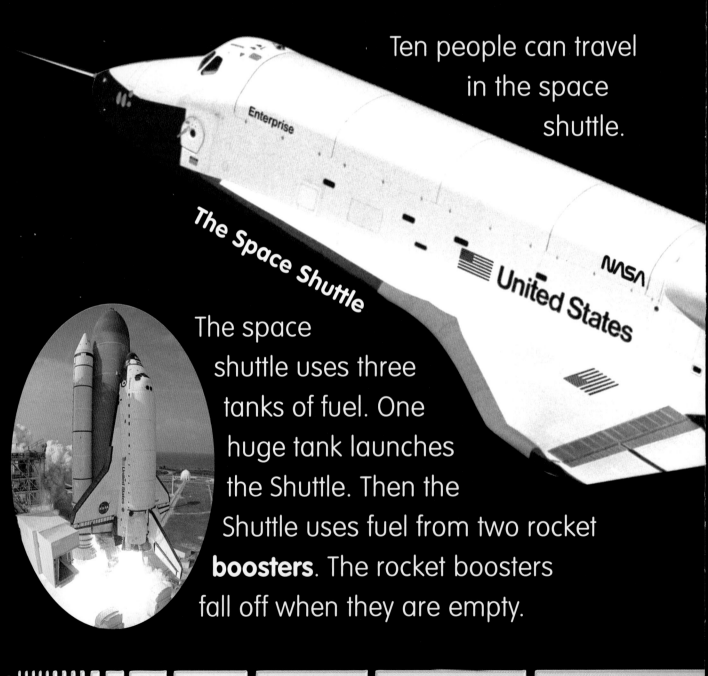

Ten people can travel in the space shuttle.

The Space Shuttle

The space shuttle uses three tanks of fuel. One huge tank launches the Shuttle. Then the Shuttle uses fuel from two rocket **boosters**. The rocket boosters fall off when they are empty.

MACHINE FACTFILE

LAUNCHED:
1981

MADE IN:
USA

WINGSPAN:
23.79 metres

LENGTH:
56.14 metres

TOP SPEED:
17,440 mph

GLOSSARY

acceleration	A change in speed – getting faster!
airliner	A large passenger plane.
aluminium	A very light metal.
Antarctica	An area of the world that is covered in ice and snow.
blades	The parts of a helicopter that spin round.
body	The outside part of a vehicle.
boosters	Fuel tanks that are fixed on to the side of a spacecraft.
brake disk	A part of a vehicle that helps to slow it down.
carbon fibre	A material that is used when a vehicle needs to be made of something strong but light.
cargo	Things carried from one place to another by a truck, plane or boat.
chamber	Another word for a room.
chute	A slide to take things from one place to another.
convertible	A car that you can drive with the roof up or down.
crew	The people who drive and work in a vehicle.
dashboard	The part of a vehicle that has displays which show how fast it is going and how much petrol it has.
engine	The part of a vehicle that burns fuel and gives it the power to move along.
exhaust	Pipes at the back of a vehicle that take away the gasses that the engine makes.

fire retardant	Something dropped onto fires to stop them spreading, such as foam or water.
flameproof	Something that won't catch fire if flames touch it.
Formula One	A famous racing competition.
four-wheel drive	A car that has power in all four wheels.
frame	The part of a bike that holds the engine and wheels together.
hood	The lid over the engine.
hull	The main part of the ship that sits in the water.
loud speaker	Makes your voice very loud when you speak into it.
mines	Places where metals and coal can be dug from the earth, or from rocks.
officers	The people in charge.
on site	The place where the work is going on.
quarries	Rocky places where rocks are excavated and taken away to be used for building.
radiator	Part of a vehicle that lets it cool down.
sensors	Things that help pilots fly the plane, fire weapons and spot enemy planes.
shovel	A scoop used to lift rocks and earth.
steel	A strong metal.
submarines	Underwater warships.
submersible	A machine that goes underwater.
suede	A furry kind of leather.
superbike	Fast road bikes that are like racing bikes.
supercar	A fast and expensive road car.
wingspan	The length between the tips of a plane's wings.

INDEX